Eliphalet Nott Potter

Discourses Commemorative of Professor Tayler Lewis

Eliphalet Nott Potter

Discourses Commemorative of Professor Tayler Lewis

ISBN/EAN: 9783337407544

Printed in Europe, USA, Canada, Australia, Japan

Cover: Foto ©Suzi / pixelio.de

More available books at **www.hansebooks.com**

DISCOURSES COMMEMORATIVE

OF

PROFESSOR TAYLER LEWIS, LL.D., L.H.D.,

Delivered at Commencement, 1877;

AND OF

PROFESSOR ISAAC W. JACKSON, LL.D.,

Delivered at Commencement, 1878.

BY

ELIPHALET NOTT POTTER, D.D., LL.D.,

President of Union University.

PUBLISHED BY REQUEST

OF THE

ALUMNI AND TRUSTEES.

TAYLER LEWIS, LL.D., L.H.D., NOTT PROFESSOR OF THE ORIENTAL LANGUAGES AND LECTURER ON BIBLICAL AND CLASSICAL LITERATURE, IN UNION COLLEGE, DEPARTED THIS LIFE ON THE ELEVENTH DAY OF MAY, 1877.

> I know that my Redeemer lives;
> And o'er my dust, Survivor, shall he stand.
> My skin all gone, this [remnant] they may rend;
> Yet from my flesh shall I Eloah see; —
> Shall see Him mine; —
> Mine eyes shall see Him — stranger now no more.
>
> Job xix, 25, 26, 27;
> *in Doctor Lewis's Rhythmical Version.*

No subject can form for us a more suggestive Baccalaureate theme than the life of the Alumnus whose career as pupil, professor and p.triot, as scholar, author and Christian gentleman, we are assembled to commemorate. And yet the biographical sketch of a great man is apt in its impression to be as unsatisfactory as are the attempted reproductions of the Alps in miniature. The relative height of mountains and depth of valleys may be given exactly, and the places of glaciers and the course of streams may be traced accurately, but the grand impression of nature is wanting.

If we portray him who is the subject of this memorial discourse with fidelity, the portrait at best will lack the power and sympathy of life.

> "Oh for the touch of a vanished hand
> And the sound of a voice that is still!"

Oh for his presence once more with us here now! But alas! that may not be.

Like Cromwell, who is said to have exclaimed to the too flattering artist, " Paint me as I am," Doctor Lewis were the last man to be fond of flattery, to have courted eulogy or permitted panegyric. And yet it is difficult to speak of him in ordinary language and as we speak of ordinary men ; for " one star differeth from another star in glory," even in that spiritual system of which Christ is the central life and light.

In the year of our Lord 1802, the honored subject of this discourse was born in this State, at Northumberland in Saratoga county. Those who have visited his birth-place and are familiar with the scenery of the upper Hudson as it flows through rich fields and fragrant meadows, with wooded hills near at hand and mountains in the distance; those who have traced along the river's bank the winding and romantic walks, shaded by noble trees — the evergreen pine and cedar predominating — can understand his life-long love for his old home, his unwearied delight in the similar scenery of this beautiful Mohawk valley and his reverent appreciation of the being of God as revealed in nature.

The time of his birth is somewhat memorable in our national annals. Peace and prosperity, to which the land had long been a stranger, had at last succeeded to the storms of the Revolution and to the partisan disturbances of early constitutional and political strife. The administration of Thomas Jefferson which began the previous year, was to continue until the year 1809. Aaron Burr was Vice-president. Napoleon, already First Consul, had extended his hand and grasped the presidency of the Italian Republics, an earnest of his limitless ambition. By the peace of Luneville and Amiens, critical and dangerous questions for the United States as to impressment and neutral rights were temporarily put at rest. But it was only for a time. The renewal of war in Europe, the aggression of belligerents upon neutral commerce, the assumption of despotic power by Napoleon in the government of France, were regarded in the United States with bitter indignation by one party, the federalists, while the aggressive and haughty policy of England was as intensely irritating to the other party in our national politics. The opposing schemes for meeting these exigencies, were soon to rekindle anew the vehemence of partisan controversy and to prepare the public mind for the war of 1812. These events occurring during the first ten or eleven years of the life of Tayler Lewis had their effect upon his impressible and precocious nature. The home and neighborhood in which he lived was one where these exciting topics were sure to be discussed. His father, an officer in the Revolutionary war, had served his country with devotion and distinction. Monmouth, Germantown, Fort Stanwix, Yorktown, and the storming of the redoubts of Cornwallis, were among the battles, sieges, patriotic fortunes he had passed. These memories, with the then fresh details, entered deeply into the young life of his son, were frequently alluded to with justifiable pride in after years and, we may well believe, were the foundation of that high, devoted and enthusiastic patriotism which was among the distinguishing characteristics of Tayler Lewis.

He was baptized in his infancy; his mother having made the long journey to Albany in several instances with a view to the baptism of her children; and she gave her son the Christian name, "Tayler," for she was a niece of Lieutenant Governor John Tayler, of

Albany. Her son was wont to speak of her as a good Christian mother devoted to her household.

The earliest testimonial to his youthful scholarship is contained in a time-worn document found among his papers, dated, " Northumberland school, July 19th, 1811," and written with the old-style precision of the day, as follows:

" This may certify that Mr. Tayler Lewis is well versed in reading, writing, English Grammar and Geography; and has obtained the rudiments of Arithmetic, commenced classical studies and made proficiencies beyond my most sanguine expectations. His good manners, disposition, and assiduity in study, highly recommend him to friends and acquaintance and to those who are friends of science." Like a quaint but life-like portrait, this shows that young Lewis already gave unconscious testimony to the truth of the poet's line, " The child is father to the man," and evinced the scholarly passion of his life in the assiduity which led his intelligent preceptor to say he commenced classical studies and made proficiencies beyond the most sanguine expectations. The preceptor long remembered his bright little scholar, and quite recently his descendants have written from the West, giving evidence of the strong impression of ability so early made. He was afterwards at school in Milton, Saratoga county. A friend, then his schoolmate, after an interval of more than half a century, recalls with deep interest characteristics similar to those here referred to.

His preparation for college was made at Salem, Washington county, under the direction of Dr. Proudfit, a man of strong character, who, like his relative, Prof. Proudfit of Union College, was affectionate and kind in his intercourse with his pupils. Doctor Lewis traced some of his earliest and deepest religious impressions to this influence; and was profitably and permanently affected, from waking in the night to find his faithful teacher and friend kneeling at his bedside and pouring out petitions for his spiritual welfare. As he was but eighteen years old when he graduated from college in 1820, and a mere boy when four years earlier he entered it, we cannot but be struck with the deep and lasting impression there made upon him. We trace his courage and patriotism to his father, the first elements of his religious life to his mother, and the impetus given to his intellectual life to his Alma Mater. Although, in his later career, he was to stand for the metaphysical rather than the physical, for the ideal rather than the practical, while President Nott, then in his prime, was eminently practical in his aims and influence, yet the spell cast upon this pupil in college days never left him. As when a pupil, so when he became a professor and finally a biographer of President Nott, he still honored, revered and loved him as in many respects the foremost man of his time, one whose memory was so dear to him that in the last days of his life he asked to be buried near Dr. Nott in the College Cemetery.

Among his classmates were Laurens P. Hickok, William H. Seward and others, destined to eminence, while some are respected citizens of this neighborhood. His room-mate, now an aged clergyman, has recently revisited the college, the room, the walks, the scenes, once enjoyed with this early friend whom in college days and ever since he has loved as a brother. This intimate acquaintance, commenced during early boyhood when prosecuting the academical course of studies, about the year 1814, was continued in college; and his room-mate during his entire course informs us that he regularly read a portion of God's word and that, generally in the early morning; nor was he backward in speaking to others of the thoughts that were thus suggested to him. His little pocket-Bible was always upon the table and numerous pencil comments were to be seen on its pages. Sometime in the year 1817, a weekly prayer meeting was organized in the section. Young Lewis was not only regular in his attendance, but took an active part in it. Slight and boyish in appearance, he was, as Dr. Hickok informs us, the best swimmer in his class and by no means neglectful of athletic exercises, although chiefly remarkable for his quiet, earnest and diligent attention to his duties.

Judge Samuel A. Foot of Geneva, who graduated from Union College in the year 1811, states that Tayler Lewis entered his office at Albany as a student of law, soon after his graduation from this Institution, and continued in the office until three years later, when he was admitted to the bar. His classmate in college, William Kent, son of the distinguished jurist, James Kent, was for a time his fellow-student in the office. So purely intellectual was young Lewis, that, when tired of his law books, his recreation was found in calculating eclipses. He had one of the clearest and most active intellects and was regarded as certain of great distinction in the practice of law. Declining a promising opening, he returned to Fort Miller and prepared to practice law in the immediate neighborhood of his birth-place. He connected himself with the Reformed Dutch church there, was one of its most efficient members and was elected a member of its consistory. His brother, who studied in his office during this period, writes that "when the cholera, small-pox or other contagious diseases prevailed, the young lawyer, unaccompanied by any ministers, would visit the sick and the dying to pray with them and administer spiritual advice and consolation." He was also brave and generous in defending without pecuniary compensation the cause of the poor, the defenceless and the oppressed.

But meanwhile he was perplexed by conscientious doubts as to his professional duties. The true direction of his future career was given, in the seemingly accidental suggestion of a clergyman interested in the Hebrew Scriptures, that he should take up the study of Hebrew. This he did with avidity. In his professional journeys, his Hebrew Bible became his constant companion. I well remember his glowing description of his deepening interest and progress in this study and in the renewal and further prosecution of his college classics; how the dawn would creep up over the hills, and the rays of the rising sun flood the valley of the Hudson, rousing this eager student to the consciousness that all through the night and far into the morning he had been pursuing those classical and Scriptural studies which he was destined to follow through life over great obstacles and on to great eminence, and which in return were to be found the source of his delight and solace in the shadow of the valley at the close of life's pilgrimage.

That pilgrimage was not made alone, for life-long friends walked onward with him. Neither was he without those domestic surroundings which were essential to a nature so loving and social and sympathetic. He was married in 1833. You may see the old homestead of his wife's family, still in their possession, standing near Fort Miller on the borders of the Hudson. I know of no more touching tribute to domestic felicity than that scene toward the close of his life, when, calling his aged wife to his side with a fond embrace, he alluded to the lovely walks along the river banks in their youth, but exclaimed of the love of these last days of earthly life, " It is even better, far better, now." Later on, after a restless night, in the stillness of the early morning, to his wife and daughter who insisted on sitting up still longer with him, he exclaimed, " Ruskin has written a great deal about art and nature, but he has never yet written anything about an old man who lies sick and suffering, with a dear old wife and devoted daughter tending him; and until he has written that, he has never written all that he should."

Soon after his marriage, influenced by his tastes and circumstances, he became principal of the Academy at Waterford. In the columns of the Waterford Atlas, when he was about thirty years of age, we find the earliest traces of his authorship. Discussing earnestly such themes as Skepticism, the Stage, Earthly Illusions, the Heavens, Religion, Intemperance, the Sin of Pride, the Relations of Church and State, the Dangers of the Republic, he wrote in a spirit which devoutly recognized the Bible as a logical power as well as a rule of action; so that he once said, " Reason commits suicide when it refuses the aid of the Bible." His style, in his earlier articles, hardly foreshadows his later power, yet they are strikingly characteristic in their reverence for religion, their elevated speculations, their practical exhortations and in the choice of themes.

He moved to Ogdensburgh, St. Lawrence county,

in the year 1835, accepting the principalship of the Academy there and writing frequently for the Ogdensburgh Times during his residence of two years; after which he returned for two years more to his old post at Waterford.

His public life dates from 1838, when, in accordance with the wish of President Nott (who had discerned the genius of his pupil), he delivered the Phi Beta Kappa oration at Union College. His subject was " Faith the Life of Science." In his treatment of the difficult and then novel theme, he showed "an acuteness of analysis, a power of generalization, and an affluence of classical learning," which justified the wide circulation achieved by the address when published. Its repetition was called for at other institutions. His consequent reputation procured for him at once the offer of several collegiate professorships. He accepted that of Greek and Latin Literature in the University of the city of New York. It is interesting to note that the Union graduate in whose office, as we have seen, he had studied law, together with his fellow-student at the bar, who was also his classmate at Union, was instrumental in securing his appointment and acceptance of this important position for which he was so well qualified.

The change to the Metropolis produced a marked effect upon the development of his character and scholarship. He could then measure himself with his peers; in place of village periodicals, the great newspapers and magazines and publishing houses of the period surrounded him and were open to him. His pupils were older and more advanced than those he had previously taught, with the alertness stimulated by city life, and an appreciation and sympathy which led, through evenings spent in scholarly intercourse, to life-long and helpful friendships. Society introduced him to converse with refined, congenial and highly cultivated minds; the University, to scholars eminent and inspiring. The great political, moral and religious interests of the community, of which he always felt himself to be a responsible member, opened to him a still wider arena. He who might have been but a selfish scholar and recluse, entered upon it as the champion of whatever he believed to be right; furnishing articles for reviews and newspapers, and delivering forcible addresses at colleges and seminaries; proving that a new individual force had entered into the higher politics of the city, State and nation.

In one of the metropolitan papers of the day he published a pungent criticism on certain public lectures which he regarded as open to the charge of disbelief in the Mosaic account of the creation. The lecturer was touched to the quick and demanded the name of his critic. Professor Lewis promptly gave his name; but "when called upon, in my office," said Judge Foot, " by a portentous relative of the lecturer, some six feet in height, who looked with surprise on the firm but frail little professor and proceeded with a demand for a recantation of some portions of the criticism, those bright, sparkling eyes fairly beamed with fire as he answered, 'Recant? No, not one word!'" The interview ended satisfactorily, however, as he readily and fully disavowed all personal ill-will or intention to injure the feelings of the lecturer or to go beyond the subject-matter of the lecture. Naturally a controversialist, whether because of his martial ancestry or no, he readily took the aggressive against whatever he believed to be erroneous, and was prompt to rebuke it, alike among friends or foes. It is the comment of an intimate friend that he was looked to as one of the readiest defenders of the church against skepticism, even while he awoke alarm by his exposure of Scriptural misinterpretation and orthodox fallacies: that he rejoiced in the strongest, not to say the most defiant, assertion of his convictions; that while his ready wit disconcerted opposition, his versatility was a match for opponents, and that these qualities making intellectual combat a source of pleasure to him, he himself realized that in controversy he did not always remain dispassionate. Writing of Farrar's Life of Christ, he says, "In some places Farrar seems too tolerant; but this may be only because he is a better Christian than I am in my harsher judgment." Still the controversialist, if he be earnest, cannot but give thrusts which wound, even as the soldier who battles must draw blood. Paul, in all ages recognized as one of the ablest of the champions of the truth, exclaims not only, "I have kept the faith," but also, "I have fought a good fight."

Professor Lewis, let us here remark, was well armed for the battle of active, earnest life, because, though unconscious of what awaited him and pursuing knowledge purely for its own sake, his leisure as well as his working hours were always well employed. His was an example harmonizing with the counsel which, when Chancellor of Union University, Governor John A. Dix gave to our graduating class as to the life-long prosecution of studies begun in college. Already the Iliad and Odyssey, the Greek drama, Plato, Aristotle; the pastoral poets and lesser Hexameter poets; Herodotus, Thucydides, Xenophon, Plutarch, Longinus, Lucian, Cicero, Virgil, Horace,

Ovid, with other classic authors, and last, but not least, the Hebrew Bible, were re-read frequently and critically. And thus it has been truly said of him that he read ancient authors in the original, instead of reading about them; the quotations and references for which he was so remarkable, being recollections or spontaneous suggestions of his own mind and not taken at second hand from note, index or lexicon.

The degree of Doctor of Laws, received while he was at the University of New York, was conferred by Union College. Although fulfilling successfully his professional engagements, prosecuting his scholarly researches and giving attention to the duties of a citizen, he was also preparing to offer to the learned and religious world a contribution worthy to be the first-fruits of nearly twenty years of toil.

In opposing the materialistic and skeptical tendencies of the times, it was natural that Doctor Lewis should turn to the great classic writer, who, centuries before the Christian era, combatted the same tendencies among the cultured and progressive men of Athens. In 1844, in his forty-second year, he published the first of his works. It was entitled, "Plato against the Atheists," and was dedicated to Doctor Nott as "President of the author's revered Alma Mater and in remembrance of the lessons of theoretical and practical wisdom," received from him. It received from scholars in this country and Europe a cordial welcome. It is only for the life-long student of Greek literature and philosophy to measure its value; but the thoughtful reader will admire its multitude of learned and apt citations from the poets and thinkers of Greece and Rome and from Hebrew writers, its subtle etymologies, its profound and sometimes beautiful disquisitions in metaphysics, and will enjoy the simplicity and clearness of the style. Plato, it will be remembered, attacks, first, those who deny God's existence, then those who deny His providence and lastly those who deny His sin-avenging justice. His commentator selects the principal points of the argument and the difficult passages and words, and gives more or less dissertation to each. He treats these topics with a just reverence for his master, with the insight of intellectual sympathy and with a sense of fellowship with those who in all ages have stood for right, duty and Godliness.

In 1849, Doctor Lewis accepted the professorship of Greek in Union College, and later, its chair of Oriental Languages and Biblical Literature. As in his former position, so here, he exerted an unusual influence, especially upon the finer minds among his pupils. In the class-room he aimed rather to interest and stimulate than to drill. To those to whom his department of instruction was congenial, contact with him was like a revelation. The classics, the Scriptures, philology, history, current events, seemed filled with new meaning. His statement of facts and events as proving the presence and purpose of a Divine Providence ordering " all things for good," the inculcation of a purer aim, a higher patriotism, scholarship and Christian manhood — who that knew him in his prime and has listened to these utterances in his class room, lecture-room, Bible-class, or in his matchless conversations, has not caught somewhat of the inspiration of his earnestness and realized the originality and power of his genius? His eye brightened, his voice rose, as he gave with rhythmic beat the noble Homeric or dramatic passages. He advised his pupils to commit these not merely by rote, but "by heart," that their influence might be lifelong. He called his students to what he had himself exemplified — the pursuit, for its own sake, of truth, knowledge and philosophy.

Here too, as from early manhood, he continued his laborious study of the Hebrew and Greek languages, literature and philosophy. He became familiar with the Rabbinical writings. He could converse easily in Greek and sometimes conducted his reflections in it. His marginal notes in books were more frequently written in Hebrew, Greek or Latin than in English. He wrote original Hebrew or Greek verse readily. To these acquirements he now added Syriac, Samaritan, Koptic, Chaldaic and Arabic; the Koran being thoroughly studied, and the Thousand and One Nights in the original furnishing him with light reading. He had some knowledge of the Gothic, and read the German and several modern languages. It is needless to say that he was master of English.

In 1855, the world of theological and scientific scholars was moved by the publication of a volume on the Creation as Revealed, maintaining that the Biblical day was not limited to twenty-four hours. His argument is mainly philological but is also metaphysical. The closeness of its logic, the breadth of its learning, the delightful surprises of etymology everywhere occurring, the relief it offered to many an earnest and doubting mind, the eloquence naturally inspired by the sublimity of the subject, well justified the attention which it received from friends and opponents. The attacks of the latter drew forth in the following year a defence of the author's position, entitled, The Bible and Science, or The World Problem. In 1860, he published The Divine

Human in the Scriptures; in the preface to which he promises a work for posthumous publication, on the Figurative Language of the Bible. Meanwhile he had supplied the editorial and other columns of many leading magazines and newspapers with an immense amount of invaluable material, welcomed by an ever-widening circle of readers.

The civil war of 1861 found him ready for his country's service. He helped forward to the field his son and son-in-law, who had taken commissions in the army. He was unwearied in patriotic appeals and arguments. He furnished a series of articles on the subject of State Sovereignty which excited great interest among the influential of all parties. He filled columns with disquisitions upon slavery and with similar discussions and appeals. Somewhat later appeared his Heroic Periods in a Nation's History. Unable to wield the sword, he wielded untiringly a pen as sharp and powerful. His "State Rights, a Photograph from the Ruins of Ancient Greece" was, without his intervention, scattered far and wide and was felt to be influential in moulding the opinions of the cultured classes. "The Union professor," wrote Charles Astor Bristed, "has studied Greek in a thoroughly practical and profitable manner. With the spirit of Greek philosophy as illustrated by Greek history, he is perhaps more thoroughly imbued than any man in the country; nay, we have little hesitation in saying that no Hellenist throughout Anglo-Saxondom has ever drawn an historical parallel so finished and telling as this Photograph."

Before the war Doctor Lewis had held, on Biblical grounds, that slavery was not in itself a forbidden institution. His characteristic conservatism kept him at first from the ranks of the abolitionists, but it soon transferred him to the advocacy of freedom for the Southern slave. He demanded the restoration of the Union and the destruction of slavery; and President Lincoln's willingness to accept the first without the last aroused his utmost indignation. When asked what we should do with the negro, he answered, " What, sir, shall the negro do with you ? With disrespect to nobody, the one question is as fair as the other." He loved the Union but was unwilling to accept it at the sacrifice of what to him was a matter of principle. In a letter to a friend after the war, he wrote, " My soul clings to the old issues not yet decided after all the blood that has been shed. It is solely a question of truth and righteousness." Horace Greeley said of him, that he had " placed Conservatism in its true light before the world and was one of those who would be more highly appreciated after decease than while they yet lived. Able, acute, and industrious, devoting not only his hours but his energies, his heart with his life, to a vindication of the claims of the Christian faith to the acceptance and reverence of scholars and thinkers, he is one of the precious few who are aiding to rescue the word Conservatism from its popular perversion to the foulest ends, and to devote it once more to the characterization of steadfast loyalty to truth and righteousness." If a conservative, Doctor Lewis was also a firm believer in human progress. " The world," he writes, " we may joyfully believe, is advancing and is destined to advance. To doubt it is to doubt the prophetic record. The world for which Christ died is not destined to ultimate barbarism or the final chaos of infidelity. The true conservative stream of religious influence must rise with renewed energy from every encounter, until, in the language of prophecy, it covers the earth with the knowledge of God." And this progress of mankind, he believed was also tending toward the realization of true catholicity in Christian unity. "In Christendom," he wrote, " separation, division, is never to be treated as a good *per se* ; the church was one in the beginning, visibly and organically one, and such it will be in the end."

In 1863, having suffered already for many years from extreme deafness, his nervous system became still farther impaired by the prolonged excitement of the war and the disasters which befell his sons in the field. The alarming wounds received by one and the sudden death in battle of the other, produced a shock which utterly destroyed his hearing and undermined his general health. But he never lost interest in the movements of society, writing for the papers on topics such as "Evolution," "Religion and Morality, etc." So late as 1872, he conducted vigorous discussions on the question of the Bible in the Public Schools. In these debates, he maintained that the State had a distinct religious responsibility, its very right to existence being not in popular consent — for he had little respect for majorities — but in the command of God.

Doctor Lewis was an interested and honored member of the University Convocation of the state of New York; and among the valuable papers which he read before it, one of the latest and most celebrated was entitled, "Classical Study; there should be more of it in our Colleges or it should be abandoned." Not that he would abandon it. By better and more extended training in preparatory schools, he hoped that college courses might yet come to be more than avenues of grammatical drill; so that through the vestibule of philology the student might thence enter the temple of ancient thought and classic philosophy. He spoke as one who, not without success, had striven to introduce his pupils to these higher realms of contemplation, and he received the thanks of scholars and the Convocation for this masterly and timely effort. From this body he received the honorary degree of L.H.D.

His closing labors would alone have been worthy of a long life. He gave three years to his translation and annotation of Genesis for Lange's Commentaries. Then followed, for the same great work, his Rhythmical Version of Ecclesiastes with notes, and then that of Job; from which I have selected his favorite passage, not so much as the text for this discourse as presenting at its outset the substance of his faith in immortality.

In 1875, appeared those lectures, delivered before the Theological School at New Brunswick, N. J., and published by order of the General Reformed Synod, in which he treats of the Fearfulness of Atheism, the Denial of the Supernatural, the Cosmical Objections (astronomical and geological) to Scripture, and the Superiority of Bible Theism to the physical or philosophical views of Cosmos. In re-affirming in these lectures and elsewhere truths for which, like those ancient writers whom he most revered, he lived and would have willingly died, how many hearts has he gladdened with the vision of the truth which fills the cold void of materialism with the loving presence of the Divine all-fatherhood! There are passages in his writings which, recalling the solemn utterances of Socrates and Plato, burn with an imagination lurid and terrible as that of Jean Paul's dreadful dream of Atheism, in which he portrays the wanderings of a despairing Christ through a Godless and crumbling universe.

It was fitting that his last public appearance should be upon the Commencement stage of his Alma Mater; and there in 1876 he delivered that address ranking in some respects among the best of his utterances, in which he congratulated his life-long friend, Doctor Jackson, upon reaching in sound heart and health the semi-centennial anniversary of his connection with the Faculty of Union College.

Not long before his death, Doctor Lewis said to me that he had made it a rule of his life to return to his Alma Mater at each Commencement — an example worthy of general imitation. For some years he drove down from Fort Miller, to Commencement. The wagon was the same, perhaps with the addition of a patch or two, in which in his college days he used to be brought here, not without some forebodings, at the opening of each term. His way towards the Commencement festivities, however, was bright with pleasant anticipations. The prospect of re-unions with college friends and instructors as well as of the literary features of the occasion attracted him. On the morning after Commencement, he started homeward to drive through the same enchanting scenery, but "*quam mutatus!*" The world looked dark and he was oppressed with a sense of sadness and dreariness as he saw the place he loved receding behind him. And having loved Union College then, he loved it unto the end. When from other quarters, after he had become a member of its Faculty, tempting offers were made him, he could not be drawn away. One of his few regrets in parting with this world was evinced in the exclamation in the last weeks of his earthly life, Oh, how can I leave Union College! His love for it, for its summer landscape, its autumnal foliage, its garden, its sunsets, even for its old buildings and its winter, was unfailing. He remembered the memorable year in his college days, when the snow fell in June and July; and during his last winter, when confined to his room, he would ask, "Is the snow piled high on the Campus?" In the opening spring, though so long insensible to sound, his question was, "Are the birds singing and the winds sounding among the trees in the College woods?"

He loved his friends and associates with peculiar constancy. The classic ideal of guest-friendship was not unlike his friendliness to his friends and friends' relatives. He condescended to men of low estate or rather his sympathies were with them as though they were his peers. Who ever did more literary labor for others without reward? He had no pride of intellect. How patient he was, with people who insisted on his examining and correcting manuscripts destined to be rejected by the publishers, or if successful with publishers and the public, owing their success to the unrecognized influence of his revisions and suggestions! If irritated, he bore malice toward none. The slave and the outcast found in him a friend. He took little children into the embrace of his scholarship with those Scriptural lessons which are taught in so many Sunday-schools and by which "he being dead yet speaketh."

His versatility and the range of his accomplishments were surprising. In the higher mathematics he worked out original problems with diligence and delight. His enthusiasm for astronomy, of which one of his earliest printed articles treats, led him often in the nights of his sickness to ask, "Is Orion shining tonight? Is he bright?" His love for music was attested by occasional compositions and by his eloquent advocacy of its early cultivation as conducive to order and beauty and to the believing spirit. After he had lost all sense of hearing, he sometimes by fingering the notes upon the key-board, sought to revive the memories of music or to trace some new musical suggestion.

His familiarity with the poets, especially with Shakespeare, was unusual. He sympathized with all phases of human life, so that (an omnivorous reader) the popular romance, or stories read in the original Arabic, or the scrap-book of olden times were alike a refreshment after intellectual labor. Keeping himself informed as to the current events, he followed with intelligent interest the progress of modern science. I have not time to quote within the limits of this discourse the copious extracts I have made from his published works and from his early fugitive efforts, terse, pregnant and foreshadowing, as we have seen, the great productions of his life. I trust that a uniform edition of his works may be projected and published, including those left by his wise forethought ready for the press, and preserving also the scattered jewels which fell so freely from his tongue and pen.

I need not in this presence describe his striking personal appearance, his noble brow, his dark piercing eye, his flowing locks, his facile hand, his alert movement.

But the mental habitudes of such a man, naturally an object of much interest to all students, young and old, are not to be passed over in silence. As one informs me, who knew him well, before the beginning of my own student-life in college and our continued intimate association in its Faculty, the Doctor was from the first an incessant worker. He never set apart a study-hour or one exclusively for recreation. I would that he had! His walks were meditations, his only excursions were excursions in the fields of thought. He was never happier than in the cloister-like quiet of his study through the long summer vacations on the College hill. With doors locked and curtains half-closed, with back square against the arm of the settee and knees drawn up to hold an Arabic folio prayer-book of the ninth century, his contentment was supreme. He often went reluctantly to his meals (not unfrequently omitting them) and returned directly to his work. Sleep was another intrusion which he resented, always sitting up late into the night and yet rising at the hour usual with the family. Acute suffering and actual loss of power convinced him, when too late, of his mistake in not recognizing and obeying the laws of health. Neglect of them injured the sense of hearing and indeed all the faculties, lessening both happiness and hopefulness.

His reading included, as we have intimated, an immense number of books, ancient and recent, on every imaginable subject; but still he would re-read one book, even a favorite fiction (such as the Arabian Nights, Romola, The Mill on the Floss), over and over again. He was very fond of history. He delighted in re-reading his Euclid in the Arabic of three centuries ago. He enjoyed broad humor as thoroughly as he did the subtlest wit; sometimes by anecdotes of blundering utterance, illustrating a nice distinction in psychology.

Keeping pace with his thoughts, his pen was always

busy, as a vast quantity of marginal and loose memoranda, attest. For forty-five years, without a day's failure, he noted down the incidents of his personal and household life, a walk, payment of a bill, arrival of letters, visitors, topics of an interesting conversation and invariably the state of the weather; although never recording his sentiments or reflections. His grief over a beloved daughter's death sought relief in the touching form of a little book of consolatory verses from the Bible, each one beautifully written out in Hebrew, Greek and Latin. His hand-writing in all languages was clear and symmetrical. He was never content with the first form of his thought or expression and seldom sent a first draught to the printer. He re-wrote the whole of Plato against the Atheists and of the Vedder Lectures, at least three times. He disliked and habitually put off letter-writing because of this necessity which he felt for accurate and full expression even on ordinary subjects. His love of symmetry led him, in arranging his books on the shelves of his library, to regard not simply their subjects but their appearance and size. His books in fact were his only indulgence, nay, his necessary companions. His library was as essential to his enjoyment as to his literary life. Many years before the semi-centennial celebration to which we have referred, it was the privilege of his old friend, Doctor Jackson, as the eldest member of the Faculty, to convey to him a pecuniary testimonial which far more than removed a distressing mortgage then resting upon this library. His surprise and gratitude were like those feelings with which upon his last birthday he received a floral tribute accompanied with loving lines from his brethren of the Faculty. He valued the sentiment and the affection, and his appreciation was as quick and natural and out-spoken as that of a child.

He was especially grateful in the former instance, because of the fact that his "scientific friends," as he was wont thereafter to call them, representing a class he had attacked with no little vehemence in his controversial writings, were among the most active in the movement which rescued his library. Its shelves bear witness, like the strata of the rocks, to the order, sequence and progress of systematic work — a library not large, but so choice and so characteristic, that his admirers and pupils would do well to secure it intact to be preserved permanently as his memorial in the College Library. For that library is to be placed, for a time at least, in the Alumni and Memorial Hall, the progress of which he watched with deep interest and for which he wrote the motto, both oriental and classical, which stands inscribed in Hebrew characters upon its dome:

> Dies brevis,
> Opus multum,
> Merces magna,
> Magister domûs urget.

> היום קצר
> המלאכה מרובה
> השכר הרבה
> האדון דוחק

The brief day drawing to its close found him still laboring for the Master, whose claims are vast but whose reward is infinite; for, his Biblical Expositions for children, though the last of his works, were, it has been remarked, as important as any; and this because of the immense numbers and peculiar impressibility of the class addressed. They were distributed monthly throughout the country. Through six months of confinement to a bed from which he never arose, they were completed according to the original plan, despite the pangs of sciatica, sleeplessness, slow wasting, and physical weakness that refused to hold the pen. With eye bright, recollection prompt and true for nearly every needed verse of the Bible or passage of an author, with reason clear and penetrating, he still wrought in his seventy-fifth year the work of many men, and such work as few at their best accomplish. During these last days, while his intellect was clear and vigorous although his frail form was thus racked with pain, he had caused to be written out and placed where his eye could constantly rest upon it, that sentence from the book of the Wisdom of Solomon:

For the corruptible body presseth down the soul, and the earthly tabernacle weigheth down the mind that museth upon many things.

On looking through the most prized volumes of his library, soon after his death, I saw written on a blank leaf in his Hebrew Bible, the following note:

"This Hebrew Bible was purchased in 1829. For a number of years, it was read through twice a-year; then once a-year and since repeatedly. Almost every difficult place has been made the subject of marginal or separate comment, every rare word noted and every rare meaning preserved in mnemonic marginal signs. It is much disfigured, but a much-studied and to me a very precious book."

This precious book and its diligent study was the foundation of his posthumous monument, destined long to endure in Biblical articles and comments and translations of the holy Scriptures, and more especially in his metrical version of the sublime book of

Job. The pages of the chapter in his Hebrew Bible, from which the text is taken, are crowded with marginal notes and references made years previous. He entered into the very spirit of the ancient collect: "Blessed Lord, who hast caused all holy Scriptures to be written for our learning; Grant that we may in such wise hear them, read, mark, learn and inwardly digest them, that by patience, and comfort of thy holy Word, we may embrace and ever hold fast the blessed hope of everlasting life, which thou hast given us in our Saviour Jesus Christ." By the thoughtfulness of a tender heart and the last tribute of a loving hand, a Hebrew psalter was buried with him, because he had often expressed his sympathy with the classic custom of placing the warrior's arms and trophies in his tomb. Even in family prayers, he always read from the Hebrew, Syriac, Greek or Latin text or from a version in a foreign tongue, rendering it fluently into admirable English. And that worn Hebrew Bible, filled with his notations, was the armory in which he was unconsciously gathering weapons for future conflict. It was the reservoir from which flowed streams making glad the people and church of God. Justly he considered the rhythmical version and annotation of Job as "the crown of all his works." And the public at large recognized the services he was rendering. His reputation is not simply local nor only national, but extends to the world of scholars and to the numberless hearts of those who love the Scriptures. It was his sincere belief that the authority of the Bible rests not simply upon a theory of inspiration but rather upon the general acceptance of, and veneration for, the book as the Word of God; so that its supreme influence upon human life and conduct must out-last all controversies about it, and all theories concerning it. His ideal of the Bible Christian was so high that, like St. Paul, some of whose traits he possessed in a remarkable degree, he would say, "I am least of all and not meet to be called a disciple of Christ, but I believe His Word, I love those who love my Lord, and my hope is in the atoning merits of Jesus as therein disclosed." An author and a reader of many books, he placed above them all, at the summit of literature, the Book of books, and regarded all knowledge but as steps leading up out of darkness to the revealed light and enduring truth of the Word of God.

Our land, the world of scholars, and Christendom itself has suffered loss. The pulpit and the press proclaim it. But as with the going down of the sun which he loved to watch from the College Campus, there are glorious traces and influences left to us.

For you, my beloved pupils who now go forth to your life-work, and for manhood and scholarship everywhere, what better lesson, what nobler incentive can there be than such a life? God speed you, every one of you, at every step of your pilgrimage! May your life and your last end be like his, whom in the brightness and beauty of the spring, pre-figuring the better life, and after the soul had craved and found release from the weary load of the body, we bore to his grave. From the solemn services conducted by those who had long known and loved him, and the eloquent words spoken by a pupil of other days, and from this sanctuary where he was wont to worship, you saw the long procession go, with solemn step and slow, bearing him to his burial, in the hope of a joyful resurrection. The gathering throng of students near his grave, the Alumni, the members of the Faculty, his friends and relatives and mourning family, the noble aspect of nature, the towering pines standing like giant warders, the hills round the College cemetery reëchoing the voices of the College choir with those of the sorrowing assemblage as they sang unitedly and touchingly the favorite hymn, " I would not live alway," the last ministries of religion, the place of burial strewn by your own hands with flowers, tokens of love and symbols of the resurrection — may the scene long be impressed upon your memories! From that open grave, may his voice seem to say to you, beloved pupil, Follow Christ, and " whatsoever thy hand findeth to do, do it with thy might."

The sun was drawing near its setting as in silence we left his burial-place. The night drew on and solitude reigned there ; but he, being forever with his Lord, was not alone ; nor was that silent grave the scene of hopeless loneliness. It was not alone, for from out the sky into which he had loved to gaze, stars looked down watchfully; not alone, for voices of Nature which he had loved and ceased to hear, whispered peace. It was not alone, for he had placed his trust in One who saith, " I will never leave thee nor forsake thee." He was not alone; but for him, rest after toil ; after battle, victory ; after separation, re-union and the fruition of his faith that it is better to depart hence and be with Christ. Said one who was near him at the last and participated in his latest and unintermitted labors, Without you, life will lose all its brightness. " But," said he earnestly, " I go where all is brightness, and you must meet me there." So may we meet him, beloved, and like him find fulfilled at the end of our pilgrimage the promise, " Be thou faithful unto death and I will give thee a crown of life."

O God, the protector of all who trust in thee; without whom nothing is strong, nothing is holy, increase and multiply upon us thy mercy, that thou being our ruler and guide, we may so pass through things temporal that we lose not finally the things eternal. Grant this, O heavenly Father, for Jesus Christ's sake our Lord. Amen.

Discourse Commemorative

of

Professor Isaac W. Jackson, LL.D.

Isaac W. Jackson, LL.D., Nott Professor of Mathematics in Union College, departed this life on the twenty-eighth day of July, 1877.

Lovely and pleasant in their lives, in their death they were not divided.

I SAMUEL, 1, 23.

A year ago we paid our tribute of respect to the memory of Professor Tayler Lewis, of whom we had but recently been bereaved; assembling then for our Commencement exercises, in the church of which he was a member. Our vacation was soon clouded by the loss of his beloved coadjutor. By custom and the courtesy of this congregation, we find ourselves now gathered, on another Commencement occasion, in the church where for more than fifty years Professor Jackson devoutly worshiped; and amid the sacred and collegiate associations of this place, it has been decided to pay to the memory of Professor Jackson likewise the tribute of collegiate service and memorial. I esteem it no light responsibility to be called upon to fulfil this duty toward one whose entire life since his graduation, for more than half a century, was devoted to this institution; a life neither eventful nor conspicuous in the world's view, presenting no such scenes or facts as those in which orators and biographers delight, yet a life most worthy of record and remembrance. For a great German writer well reminds us that we should honor most highly those who labor faithfully in class-rooms, since, although they may fall from notice like the spring blossoms, yet like the spring blossoms they live and die that fruit may be borne. It is no light responsibility, then, to speak on such a theme and at the same time to reëcho the solemn tones in which God is calling to us all from the graves of so many others connected with the College who have gone from earth within this collegiate year — intimate friends of Professors Lewis and Jackson, Trustees and former members of this Faculty. The invaluable services rendered to Alma Mater by many of them, and circumstances of peculiar interest in the career of others, call for a fuller memorial than can here be offered.

Prominent among them, was the late Mr. James Brown, who, at the time of his death and for more than thirty years previous, was a Trustee of Union College. He attested his confidence in this institution and his interest in its permanent welfare, by recent gifts and endowments amounting to one hundred and ten thousand dollars. He was a man of elevated Christian character and an exemplar of commercial honor and success. His charities were great even compared with the great fortune he amassed. His word was, in all parts of the world, a guarantee of sound and unlimited credit. He placed his talents, experience and means at the service of this institution, of which he was an honored counsellor.

Two others who have just entered into rest, the Hon. Professor Joel Benedict Nott and the Rev. Professor John Nott, had been members of this Faculty. The first was an officer of Union College from the year 1820 to 1831; a man of rare accomplishments of mind and manners, of whom his friend Professor

Joseph Henry remarked, " We scientific men suffered a great loss when he left us." Having served the College and the country with loyalty and ability, he devoted his latest studies to the elucidation of the Holy Scriptures. His brother, Professor John Nott, was an officer of the College from 1830 to 1854, deeply interested in the students and familiarly associating with them, modest, charitable, a simple-hearted clergyman, an enthusiastic teacher and an unfailing friend. As contemporary with the latter in our Faculty, we may here refer to the lamented Professor J. Louis Tellkampf, J.U.D., who departed this life a few months before Professor Jackson and was his friend and correspondent. His accomplishments, learning and rare modesty and amiability are still recalled by the older members of our College circle. He left us to return to his native Germany; and through late years he occupied with distinction a Law Professorship in the University of Breslau, a seat in the Imperial Parliament and Council and a high position among German writers on Political Economy. He always cherished grateful recollections of Union College, welcomed to his home any one associated with it and entertained bright anticipations of its future.

The Hon. John V. L. Pruyn, LL.D., connected with us as an honorary Alumnus, an invaluable adviser in the preparation of the charter of Union University and also by addresses delivered here on many important occasions, is deeply missed from the Chancellorship of the University of New York, from the Board of Regents and from many other prominent positions of public usefulness. Among the wealthy and distinguished of our own country, the eminent in Church and State from foreign lands, and among the hundreds of our toiling teachers who enjoyed frequent and cordial invitations to his home, he will long be remembered as conspicuous for a Christian grace, rarer now than of old, in that he was "given to hospitality."

The Hon. William F. Allen, recently departed, was a class-mate of Professor Jackson, and from first to last it could be said of him with truth that he was "lovely and pleasant in his life." The Bench and the Bar, the Press, the College, the Church have done honor to his exalted station and reputation and to his Christian faith. We knew him here alike to honor and to love him. When, hesitating to accept the presidency of this College, I turned to its prominent friends for counsel, Judge Allen assured me most earnestly that he sympathized with one upon whom, as he felt, so many unusual difficulties, anxious cares and arduous responsibilities were to be thrown and that I could command his best and constant efforts. No father could have been a wiser or more affectionate counsellor. Prudent in resolve, tenacious of purpose, efficient in execution, abhorring crooked ways and of unbending integrity, he was a rock of strength for our College.

Of the younger Alumni also, there are several who, closely associated with Professor Jackson here, in the year of their death are not divided from him. Of those thus departed, in whom he was especially interested, were Edward C. Taintor, a member of the class of 1863, who won early in his course the Nott prize scholarship and during his long official residence in China sent to our learned Societies valuable contributions in Oriental Philology; Grenville Tremain who presented the resolutions at the Alumni celebration in Doctor Jackson's honor and whose brief but brilliant career has just terminated; and Betaz Bröckelmann of the class of 1876. It seems but yesterday that this youngest of the departed was with us, his warm heart full of hope and his active spirit seeking a field of enterprise in the West. His bright prospects, his love for his family, his friends and Alma Mater, all are now shrouded in the blackness of a mysterious and fearful tragedy! My hand almost refuses to record the fact and my voice would fain be still; but the very memory of Doctor Jackson, answering the promptings of my own heart, assures me that he never would have passed in silence an event so full of admonition to us all. When the story of his assassination reached Germany, from her distant home in Heidelberg his mother wrote: "What shall I say in the agony of my soul? Shall I ever be able to realize this cruel fact? O Lord! why didst thou not hinder the arm of the slayer? How can I bear it, that he should end thus? my good and noble son, the joy and pride of my heart, the crown of my children, my proud, beautiful boy so cruelly dealt with. My inward eye sees the vast, endless solitude of those western plains and the lonely spot where lies my bleeding child, with his last cry to his Lord and to his mother. How can a mother's heart bear this and live and not die? Night and day, I cry unto the Lord for help not to doubt His love and to keep faith to the end. His last letter is written when he is worn out with weeks of travelling; still he writes to me, his mother, his last sign of love. I could speak forever of my own dear, faithful son, but my heart aches so, and tears almost blindfold me. God bless you." With submission to an inscrutable Providence I here denounce the "deep damnation of his taking off." I echo the question of a near relative of his abroad, Can it be that while our western emigration is the nation's hope, our general government does not prevent nor even pursue such outrages as this, especially where local authority is necessarily weak and intermittent and where private efforts at their best are utterly inadequate? And shall our country be called, as once was Spain — a land where law protects not life?

Of others in the long annual list of deceased graduates, time forbids me speak. Their memory will be duly honored on the Alumni day. We turn now to trace, so far as the limits of this discourse permit, the career of our lamented Professor Jackson.

From the quaint memorial of Isaac Jackson and his wife, the first of the family who settled in this country, we learn that previously they were resident in England and were esteemed members of the Society of Friends; and that they were about sixty years old when they thought seriously of America as their future home. They were "under exercise and concern of mind" regarding the undertaking; since Isaac, inspired perhaps by the Scriptural imagery of the new earth and new heaven with the fair river and tree and healing leaves of the Apocalypse, dreamed a dream of landing in the new world, of entering a beautiful vale through which, fed by a crystal spring, ran "a pleasant stream with hills of fair prospect on either hand." It is added that, at first a seeming wilderness, the vision changed and it became the homestead of succeeding generations of his family. Thus influenced, he embarked and landed with his household on the eleventh of September, 1725, near New Garden, Pennsylvania. After relatting his dream, he was directed by friends to an unoccupied tract near by, which to his wonder resembled closely the pleasant valley of his vision. Assisted by stalwart sons he soon established a comfortable homestead. His grandsons devoted a portion of the adjoining tract to a botanical garden, and a great-grandson further improved it by plantations of evergreens and deciduous trees now forming a somewhat noted grove. The garden ranked at that period among the first botanical gardens of the country. It is an interesting question for the student of heredity, how far we may attribute to a strain in the blood that taste for landscape-gardening and horticulture which resulted so happily for our College in the adornment of its garden, which with vale and brook and hillside-spring resembles so remarkably that of the ancestral dream.

Professor Jackson has left on record a brief but interesting estimate of the family as "honest, industrious, sufficiently-enterprising, God-fearing, God-loving people, with very few 'Honorables' so-called among them and not a single millionnaire; men and women discharging the providential responsibilities of their several stations in a manner satisfactory even to that good man who, in a community where all were honest, was commonly called by his friends and neighbors, honest William Jackson."

From this God-fearing, honest and sufficiently prosperous stock, was born at Cornwall, Orange county, in this State, on the twenty-eighth of August, in the year 1804, the son who received the old family name of Isaac and whom we have known as Professor Isaac W. Jackson. Both of his parents were members of the Society of Friends. The scenery of the neighborhood, which early made its impression upon him, was as beautiful and striking as that which had welcomed upon landing in America the forefather after whom he was named. In his childhood and during the long life of his honored mother, he was a faithful and devoted son. The talents which he manifested in his early youth induced his friends to send him from home, to secure the best advantages of academic education. He had a taste for mathematics and mechanics which was not unusual in the family, one of his uncles having invented a method in logarithms; while an old clock, bearing the family name and an early date, is still preserved, both as a memento of its maker and as an excellent time-piece. His interest and progress in his studies were such that after receiving the ordinary schooling of the vicinity he was sent in his seventeenth year to the Albany Academy.

"The first knowledge I had of my old friend," wrote Doctor Lewis, "— I may call him so, though a number of years my junior — was in the city of Albany in 1823. I was then a law-student, he a boy in the Academy. Two things drew to him more than the usual notice. One was his youthful Quaker coat, and the other the distinction of being even at that time a most superior mathematician. I must not omit a third fact that brought him — boy as he was — before the public eye. At that period when Albany was an intensely Federal city, there predominated in the Legislature a peculiar species of Democrats called Bucktails. The name is to be found in ancient newspaper files though the variety itself has long since been extinct and fossilized. They had ventured upon the hazardous political stratagem of ejecting De Witt Clinton from the office of Canal Commissioner, although the very creator of the canal policy. It was too much for our youthful mathematician, absorbed as he was in geometry and logarithms. He made the outrage the theme of his public academic exercise and exposed the atrocious meanness of the transaction in a most 'scathing Philippic,' as our sensational reporters say. The public prints took special notice of it. It became an exciting subject of conversation throughout the city; and its stripling of an author, if I am not mistaken, was in some peril of being brought before the senate on a 'question of privilege.' I mention the incident as showing what the indignant orator might have become, had he devoted himself to politics instead of the higher pursuits with which his intellectual life has been occupied."

Having completed his studies at the Academy with the highest honors both in the classics and mathematics, he entered Union College, where he attained high standing in the classics and from which in 1826, in his twenty-second year, he graduated with the first honors in mathematics and chemistry. He was at once appointed a Tutor in the College. Here, as at the Academy, it was evident that he possessed characteristics hardly compatible with the quiet spirit of Quakerism. He became actively interested in military drill and, having been chosen captain of the College company, retained that position long after graduation. Alumni fond of praising the good old times remind us that the "Captain" received his commission from President Nott in the summer of 1828 after unanimous election to the post by Company A of the Union College Cadets; and that he was promoted, receiving the title of Major; "but as no later title nor achievement of the First Napoleon could displace in the hearts of his soldiers that of 'The Little Corporal,' so, not that brilliant manœuvre which scaled the heights of Catskill under the fire of a July sun nor the triumphant march upon Fort

William Henry and ultimately to the gates of the Capitol could give our Major any prouder and dearer title with his 'boys,' than that of 'Captain.'" "Marshalling the classes for that well-ordered procession of Commencement, what a figure he used to make in those days! Some remains of the Quaker style of dress still accompanying the military show, and the flourishing of the Grand Marshal's baton, gave it an appearance as picturesque as it was original." In his later years, Doctor Jackson pointed often to the improved bodily vigor, carriage and manners of the students, as indicating the wisdom of the system of military drill and physical culture. He rejoiced towards the close of his life to see the system successfully revived and he seconded cordially the efforts of the military officer detailed by the General Government for this duty. He watched the erection of our large gymnasium with interest, since he held that the College cannot fulfil its duty without sending forth into the battle of life graduates trained in body as well as in mind. His garden was a source of health and prolonged life to him and showed the advantage of exercise in the open air and of an interest outside the routine of a profession. Yet he was far from giving undue prominence to physical, when contrasted with intellectual culture. Intellectual labor rather than rest, was the rule of his life. Friends sometimes warned him against overwork and it may be thought that, had he labored less, he might have lived even longer. Possibly, and his life from the beginning to the end of it might have been of little value to any one. Intellectual as well as physical toil is healthful; labor is life, long life often, honorable and useful life. The instances — and they are many among graduates of this College besides Seward, Lewis and himself—in which the slight and frugal toilers wore out and distanced men more muscular but less intellectually active, these instances suggest that enthusiasm for physical training should not surpass that for intellectual culture. Canon Kingsley, the noble advocate of Muscular Christianity as it has been called, scarce lived out half his days; and from the career of Dickens and of others physically as active, we are led to conclude that over-excitement and those twin emissaries of Satan, hurry and worry, are greater enemies to the longevity of brain-workers than the most intense, industrious, recluse, yet regular and frugal, life.

In this connection we may recall the fact that during his college course, with the coöperation of a band of congenial companions, some of whom have since attained to positions of eminent usefulness—among them Orlando Meads, LL.D., and Thomas Hun, M.D., LL.D.—he founded and maintained a society for social and literary purposes. In succeeding years, other like associations were formed; and hence Union College has been called the mother of the Greek-letter secret societies of the country. Doctor Jackson felt that the confidences of friendship, like the confidences of the family, though secret, may be none the less innocent; and the older he grew the more confident he became that a useful and salutary method had been devised by which College students might have such enjoyment as they craved, without violating the canons of morality or religion; the grave and the gay in temperament being mutually benefited, while the oldest College officer and graduate as well as the youngest might enter into close relations of confidence and friendship with undergraduates. Youths in the stage of life most needing the cordial intimacy of elder friends that they may receive in the right spirit their cautious and counsels, often lose these blessings through supposed lack of sympathy or because of artificial barriers. Professor Jackson hoped to remedy this evil by an association of younger and older members, both undergraduates and Alumni, who should be inspired by brotherly sentiments like those of home and church. Whatever be the counter-arguments and whether or not he builded in his youth better than he knew, such was the institution of the Greek-letter secret society in his conception of it; and as he believed, such was it to a great extent in its development. Hopeful and warm-hearted sentiments, characteristic of the man and which every member of such a society should strive to realize!

He was promoted to the Professorship of Mathematics in the year 1831. His section, comprising in accordance with our College system the rooms of the students under his more immediate charge, adjoined his residence or rather, by the construction of the building, formed part of it. He treated these students as responsible to himself mainly and like members of his family. He had access to their rooms at all times of the day and night, and his visits were frequent and friendly. He would turn the point of ill nature by a well-timed joke and meet serious wrong-doing with fatherly expostulation. Kind to the erring, he could crush vice relentlessly; and under the easy companionship which disarmed opposition, were the firmness and strength which gained the desired end. In his class-room, those were taught the topics of the text-book who desired to learn them; and those who in addition desired to solve the abstruse problems of higher mathematics, found that his clear and powerful intellect elucidated each step of the most obscure processes and conclusions.

Professor Foster states that when sent to "Captain Jackson" for his entrance-examination in algebra, having given much more study to the classics than to mathematics, he found himself with several pairs of excited nerves in the august presence. The questions proposed were more comprehensive than numerous; What were the rules? and Why were they thus? On this latter point the old school text-book had been grandly reticent. Its readers should receive the rules as objects for faith and not for vain curiosity as to their source or the reasoning upon which they had been founded. The captain graciously considered these facts, admitted the plea based upon them in bar of adverse judgment, but accompanied the desired certificate with a gentle intimation that he regarded the recipient as not well grounded; as an unprincipled youth, in fact, who would do well at the earliest possible moment to make the acquaintance of some author who would condescend to give reasons for his rules. The advice was not given in vain.

When students were indisposed or unable to grasp the mathematical problems and principles of the text-book, it was seen that he was indeed no pedagogue, but an educator inspiring mental activity by indirect suggestion. He published books on Trigonometry, Optics, Conic Sections and Mechanics, which were adopted in American colleges and in one important British institution; one of these works drawing from a competent authority the remark that he could not wish a single sentence changed; but in these productions Professor Jackson had no view to reputation; he based them on the observed needs of his classes and designed them directly for their help. The obituary record of the Faculty well declares, that, thoroughly conversant with that inductive method by the employment of which so large a portion of our knowledge has been obtained, he delighted in familiarizing his pupils with its principles and in illustrating its application to the discovery of new facts.

As an executive officer of the College he was prompt, energetic, ever watchful and active, selecting his measures judiciously and pursuing them with discretion. The severity of his earlier conceptions of discipline was modified by the influence of one whom he loved and assisted most faithfully — the late President Nott — and whom he revered as "the majestic man, the first of college presidents, the true founder and guardian genius of this institution." Whatever there may have been of severity and impetuosity in his nature, was at length mellowed through experience, inborn kindliness and Christian charity, until at last nothing so marked the man as forbearance with youth, tender oversight and friendly counsel; traits which won from his students a regard ripening with years into abiding respect and love. Thus in presenting him with a beautiful token of esteem, a number of his former pupils improved the occasion to say that "they cannot express their high appreciation of the great-hearted man whose long life of usefulness has been so filled with beauty and whose unwavering kindness contributed so much to make their college days a joyful recollection." He could be patient with the exuberance of youthful spirits and even with seeming disregard of his wishes and seeming disrespect toward himself. How many have testified to the long-suffering patience and encouraging counsel with which he sought to reclaim the erring! This Christian spirit, the growth of years of experience and patient endeavor, is one which we who are members of this Faculty may all well emulate.

In his family as well as in general intercourse, he was social and genial. Often in the evenings, coming out from his study to the drawing-room, he contributed his share of entertainment by reading aloud or by his cheerful and instructive conversation. When absent he wrote daily to those at home. He was interested in the progress and watchful of the health and education of his children. In my childhood, with an instinctive appreciation of his filial devotion I have often watched him wheeling along the garden-chair which he had devised for the comfort of his aged mother, delighting in her enjoyment of the scene and pointing out the beauties of flower-bed, lawn or grove, which he kept and dressed with unceasing care.

He was always neatly and simply attired; slight in form, well-built and active, with clear, piercing eye looking out from under a large and prominent brow; his head finely developed; his voice frank and friendly as he welcomed one to his study or garden. And that garden played no small part in extending the reputation and influence of the College. It is said that before the present excellent equipment in apparatus for the several departments was acquired, President Nott used to invite the inquiring visitor to call on Professor Jackson and to walk through the garden; thus not only producing a pleasant general impression of the College, but emphasizing the beauty, healthfulness and capabilities of its situation. The cordial reception given by Professor Jackson but exemplified the spirit of hospitality for which the College was distinguished.

His household gave ample proof of the presence of an efficient and cultured helpmeet. It was the prized resort of a large and cultivated circle of relatives and friends from abroad. During Commencement week especially, "open house" was kept and students and returning graduates found a hearty welcome. The importance of such hospitality in attracting youth to the institution and in moulding and refining student-life — especially with that controlling portion of the public who value the elegant amenities of society — cannot be over-estimated. No matter what one's intellectual gifts and efforts, he suffers great disadvantages in the race of life without some share of these graces. We may well hold, with Bacon in his Advancement of Learning, that while behavior or " the Wisdom of Conversation ought not to be overmuch affected, much less ought it to be despised; for it hath not only honor in itself but an influence also with business and government. The poet saith, Nec vultu destrue verba tua. A man may destroy the force of his words with his countenance; so may he of his deeds. Saith Cicero, recommending to his brother affability and easy access, Nil interest habere ostiam apertam, vultum clausum. And if the government of the countenance be of such effect, much more is that of speech and other carriage appertaining to conversation; the true model whereof seemeth to me well expressed by Livy, though not meant for this purpose : Ne aut arrogans videar, aut obnoxius; quorum alterum est alienæ libertatis obliti, alterum suæ."

Doctor Jackson's table was noted, if for its simplicity yet also for its excellence, as Professor Lewis reminded us in his reminiscences at the semi-centennial celebration; and many another favored friend has remembered the College through the same pleasant association. He coöperated with those sensible and philanthropic men and women who are striving to popularize economical, healthful and palatable cookery. He often purchased the works and tested the methods of those who seek so to educate poor and rich alike that the dinner, whether of herbs or of the stalled ox, may have good digestion, health and content therewith.

The salaries of collegiate professors are often declared to be too small to permit their enjoyment of the elegancies or even of the comforts of life and the pleasures of charity to the needy. But although Professor Jackson's means were very limited, his home, as we have seen, was a model of hospitality, and his charities, although at the cost of self-denial, were abundant. He indulged also for "our four-footed friends" — the comfortable old horse, the graceful hound, and other animals dear to his domestic circle — a care that would have satisfied the heart of their public champion Mr. Bergh. In addition to these objects, he contributed from his own means toward the maintenance of his beloved garden, expending on its construction and embellishment — as he stated privately a short time before his decease — from first to last a sum of about ten thousand dollars. On commencing his residence in the College building, he found a few beds of poor flowers or vegetables and, adjoining them, a rude, tangled vale. He left a garden well-ordered, widely extended, filled with select plants, shrubs and flowers, the long, shady rambles and sun-lit glades of which became one of the most attractive possessions of the College. He cultivated over three hundred varieties of roses, corresponded and exchanged with the best horticulturists of England and America, improved many species and distributed far and wide the new seeds; thus laying this State especially under great material obligations in ways not recognized. A household and its surroundings managed thus shows what a good heart, clear judgment and diligent hand can accomplish with slender means; and it further shows that in the exemption from extravagant expenditures, in the regularity of even a meagre stipend, in the comparative permanence and the social influence of our professorial positions and in the opportunities for culture and usefulness, there are compensations which may well attract the best character and talent of the times.

It is needless here to say that the science and art of horticulture were a delight and solace of the Professor's life. Valuable works on this subject make up a large part of his library. His affection for his shrubs and flowers was like that manifested by old Erasmus Darwin in his quaint poem on the "Loves of the Plants;" new varieties grew as if by magic beneath his hands. The bowers and walks of his creation became familiar haunts, lit up by the joyous presence of youths and maidens and troops of children, while often the old came halting back to revive once more the memories and emotions of other days. These grounds having been committed to his care and improved and extended during a long period by his own hand, he learned with pleasure in the last year of his life that a fund had been projected for continuing his work. He could receive no more appropriate memorial tribute.

His life centered in and was mainly bounded by his College. It was passed in his family circle, his study, his class-room or with members of the Faculty. He avoided occasions of personal prominence. When the degree of Doctor of Laws was conferred upon him by Hobart College, his modesty led him to hesitate before accepting it. In social intercourse he considerately turned the conversation toward the interests of others rather than his own, drawing them out pleasantly and speaking of subjects which they could discuss to advantage. He always expressed himself with clearness and simplicity and often with elegance. While he wrote readily, he reviewed his diction carefully and altered and polished it until acceptable to his critical taste. His diary, his study, his household and all his affairs, whether relatively great or small, show that he was determined to do whatever he attempted, as well as he could. His intellectual concentration and perseverance were such that he could not rest satisfied until he had completed what he had deliberately undertaken. Conscientious and regular in his attendance upon public worship, yet as to his personal feelings and meditations upon religion and other sacred topics he was characterized by a Quaker-like reticence, which however never prevented him at the critical moment from speaking and acting boldly for the right. He was always sympathetic, especially so with the sorrowing and the needy. Professor Henry of the Smithsonian Institute, an honorary Alumnus of this Institution, who was his fellow-student in boyhood and his life-long correspondent, said that he was "the truest and most generous soul he ever knew." His charities were from the heart as well as from the hand and he concealed their objects and extent. A nervous system extremely sensitive to physical pain and moral excitements might cause at times a certain irritability or impatience of manner, but the soul, the true man, was patient and forbearing even to tenderness. More than most men of his time, he possessed a trait which, a thoughtful observer has remarked, is, of all the moral qualities, the one becoming most rare — childlikeness, genuine simplicity of character and a modest fearlessness; such as Goldsmith and Wordsworth sometimes manifested, such as Hans Christian Andersen possessed to a fault and Ruskin has at times evinced as a mild radiance relieving periods of storm and change. Doctor Jackson felt with Doctor Lewis that the humble faith of some childlike believer elucidates at times the meaning of God's word more clearly than the learning of the undevout scholar. In his case as in that of his friend Doctor Lewis, to a life of good works was joined a life of simple, Christian faith. He had no sympathy with that scientific pharisaism which, in the search after impossible certainty, reaches the creed of universal nihilism; nor with such boasted positivism as that which forbids belief in anything we cannot see or feel or fathom, like a blind prisoner beating his body against the cold walls and bars of his narrow cell and calling out madly, Only the tangible exists; only that which I feel or handle or comprehend is positive; faith is a falsehood; beyond the limits of my narrow cell, there is nothing, no orbs of light, no nobler modes of life, no spiritual truths, no immortality, no Heaven, no God!

Fulfilling the duties of his position ably, faithfully, contentedly, no achievements of wealth or fame could have brought him wider usefulness or higher happiness ; for thousands of the educated men of the country attest their gratitude for his aid in the development of mind and character.

No less noticeable was his high appreciation of order and beauty in the natural and in the moral world, his discriminating delight in the best literature, ancient and modern, his love of justice, and his sympathy with the oppressed. Doctor Jackson's view of life in· the retrospect was like that so strikingly expressed by the Rt. Honorable Mr. Gladstone, in his letter regretting his inability to address us as Honorary Chancellor of Union University : — " I have but one complaint to make : life is too full, time too rapid ; which in truth means that the provision Divinely made for our exercise and growth is too bounteous. But it produces a relative penury of power to do the duties that are waiting and crying out to be done."

The civil war roused his patriotic heart to the highest enthusiasm. Like his ancestors, who had suffered loss of all things for conscience' sake, possessing the courage of his convictions, he manifested an impetuous fervor of attack upon whatever excited righteous indignation. His sense of honor and his moral rectitude made him impatient of false assumption and indignant at persistence in oppression and wrong. He was always an open foe, withstanding his opponent to his face. He cordially approved of the enlistment of his son William, a man of rare ability, presence and personal magnetism; and when, a sacrifice to his country's cause, his loved remains were brought home, Doctor Jackson received them with unmurmuring submission and followed them to the grave with Christian resignation. In no conventional sense but with the true spirit of patriotic devotion, he traced as the inscription for the granite monument of his son words familiar but immortal, at once classical in language and Christ-like in sentiment of self-sacrifice :

Dulce et decorum est pro patriâ mori.

At the close of the war for the Union, while the country at the north was prosperous, Union College was felt to be in a critical condition, declining steadily during many years in prestige, influence and numbers. Doctor Jackson was among the first to comprehend the situation. The institution having depended for more than half a century for its endowment and success upon one man of exceptional genius, it was requisite for its future usefulness that it should no longer be dependent upon any one alone, but that a broader foundation should be sought in the sympathy, influence and watchful care of its Alumni and of all others naturally interested in its well-being. Having been founded upon the principles of Christian unity, Union College, lacking denominational support, had claims upon the yet broader patronage of all desiring the fulfilment of our Lord's high-priestly prayer for unity; and might also turn hopefully to the unusual number of influential and successful men in all parts of the land to whom she had given efficient practical as well as literary training. Professor Jackson therefore sent forth ringing appeals to the graduates to organize local Alumni Associations. Not content with circulars or stereotyped forms of address, he wrote with his own hand letter upon letter, studying the character of all who had been his pupils, seeking how most effectually to move each one of them and resting not, day nor night, until hearty affirmative responses poured in from all quarters. On the memorable evening of April twenty-seventh, 1869, telegraphic greetings flew to Union College from New York and the principal cities of the State, and from the East and West and South, laden with the cordial expressions of the Alumni gathered at their banquets. They abounded in the warmest expressions of devotion to Alma Mater and to Piofessor Jackson, her representative on the occasion. The excellence of the addresses, the eminence of the speakers, the character of the representative Alumni, the simultaneous outburst of loyalty, made the movement as conspicuously useful and admirable as it was unparalleled. But unfortunately, it was believed at the same time and widely proclaimed that the College was richer than any of her children and needed no aid but their sympathy and influence. The fever of development of real estate following the war ran high. The Trust in land provided by Doctor Nott was considered of vast value if only held for further improvements and rise in prices. Thus the moment for immediate profitable sale or lease slipped by; the high tide in the liberal endowment of educational institutions needing and making known their needs, also slipped by without the requisite effort for this College. It was not long before this mistake began to be felt. Doctor Jackson lived to see with deep anxiety the depreciation of the unproductive and heavily assessed estate which chiefly composed the property of the institution.

When I was invited to take the Presidency of the College, Doctor Jackson urged my acceptance as a duty. After several interviews it was arranged that, devolving upon its efficient Faculty much connected with the ordinary routine of the College, the in-coming President should carry foward undertakings long since begun; such as the increase of the Library, the completion of the Alumni Hall, the provision of special facilities for the several departments together with the increase of the means for general culture. But the yearly support of the College; the increase of its regular income to meet proper salaries and other usual expenditures; provision against deficiencies until the real-estate investments could be improved; and endowments for general and ordinary purposes; this was rightly the broad field for the efforts of Trustees, Alumni, Faculty, citizens and friends of Christian unity and of education. Professor Jackson was convinced, and the history of Colleges shows his sagacity, that the continuous power of such corporations depends upon the efforts of the many as well as the devotion of a few, upon all friends interested in education and especially upon the Alumni. Knowing that while the individual dies institutions survive, he sought for the College a life not individual or circumscribed but widely expanded. He was willing to work and wait for such an era. The College would thus gain a responsible, perpetual constituency, active for its honor, its usefulness and its progress.

Doctor Jackson saw with gratitude more than three hundred thousand dollars secured, mainly toward those objects — buildings, Library and scholarships — to which the efforts of the President had been directed; he knew this sum to exceed in amount all our educational Funds or Trusts acquired during the previous three-quarters of a century except the Nott Trust now yielding but little for College purposes. That sum, however, was not larger than the outlay in a single year of some of our prominent competitors. Meanwhile, this institution had no share in the Congressional land-grants; and the many new colleges and universities were dividing college patronage and adding costly attractions. Doctor Jackson therefore earnestly desired the furtherance of the definite though not inflexible plan by which it was hoped to maintain Union in its just position among its peers. The incorporation in 1876 of Union University — the idea of which had long slumbered in our charter — was a portion of that plan. He wrote of it in the first University catalogue: "Union College acquired, by its charter, full university powers; but the creation of post-graduate institutions at Schenectady had not been found practicable. Schools of Law and Medicine and also an Astronomical Observatory had long existed at Albany, the distance between which city and Schenectady, estimated in time, is less than that which in many cases separates the professional schools from the other departments of a university. The arrangement naturally suggested by these circumstances was that the professional schools and the Observatory at Albany should be united with Union College. The union of the several institutions — although each will continue to hold its own rights, properties and Trusts as heretofore — was consummated by the incorporation, for university purposes, of Union University."

Doctor Jackson learned with approval that the resources at command would be henceforth devoted to the educational departments. He saw with satisfaction the raising of the standard of scholarship and the actual improvement under it, and a total increase in numbers despite losses through greater rigor of examinations. He concurred in discouraging the prevalent tendency to luxury and extravagance which, alien to the spirit of our national institutions and to the college usages of earlier times, has never found a place at Union; a tendency which threatens to injure the sons of the rich and to exclude or mortify the sons of the poor. He would have seen their college days characterized by simple habits and by enthusiasm for educational rather than social objects.

If we admit with Lord Chatham that confidence is a plant of slow growth, and with Doctor Jackson that after the " trials of the last quarter-century those laboring for the College have before them an arduous task," yet with him we have faith in her motto, "Perseverantia vincit; " and we believe that her trials were designed to disclose alike her needs and her resources, so that upon the broader foundation may stand the superstructure of enduring success.

Doctor Jackson had been deeply interested in the war for the Union; but when at its close he longed for peace and for the cessation of all sectional animosities, he thought it a most happy omen that among the first considerable endowments secured was one designed mainly (though not exclusively) for the benefit of students from the southern States and meeting many of the expenses incident to their residence at College; at the same time, bringing the North and the South into friendly contact and thus perpetuating the influence of one who loved both national and Christian unity. I allude to the John David Wolfe Scholarships Foundation, of fifty thousand dollars, the gift of filial affection in memory of one of New York's most benevolent merchant princes.

The culmination of Doctor Jackson's career was in 1876, at the semi-centennial anniversary of his connection with the College. Can we forget the scene? the hundreds of graduates gathering from all parts of the land; the Memorial Hall ringing with cheers of welcome and with his praises; his modesty at the banquet of the Alumni of which he was the honored guest; and how, on the Commencement morning, his dear friend, Doctor Lewis, spoke as the old man eloquent to the old man grand and true? Recalling his acquaintance with him in his youth as inspiring an admiration which deepened into the friendship of a lifetime, Doctor Lewis's voice grew strong and clear as he said, " He has lived a most useful and honorable life. It must have been a happy one. To say nothing here of that all-transcending element of the Divine grace, in which, I trust, he has been a sharer, he has had a clear mind constantly gazing upon the science of certainty, as it may be called, in contrast with the dimness and doubt and shadow that rest upon almost all the provinces of human thought. To this, has been added the most charming of outward pursuits. I refer to his cultivation, for so many years, of that beautiful garden we are all so fond of visiting. It must have been a happy life. Surely may we congratulate him on having possessed two such elements of physical and intellectual serenity. His life belongs to the past and has nothing to fear for the future. Of the love of his classes, he is sure. The warm esteem of every one who has ever sat under his teaching, the unfeigned respect of all who have ever been his colleagues, this is his literary inheritance as long as Union College holds a place among the institutions of our land; and may that be as long as our land holds its place among the nations of the earth!" As Doctor Lewis ceased, he stood where I now stand; and Doctor Jackson, rising from his seat beside him, acknowledged with the warm grasp of his hand the loving greeting of his old friend and coadjutor. Thus lovely and pleasant in their lives, it was fitting that in death they should not be divided.

What changes in history, letters, society and in the institutions and industries of this country and in the material, educational and religious interests of the world at large occurred during the span of this one life, which, just as he became conscious of failing powers, ebbed tranquilly away in sleep!

It was in the bright sunlight of a summer afternoon, in the garden, which by his care had just reached its most perfect condition, and under the great elm which he loved, that his friends gathered for funeral rites befitting the departed. It is a usage of the Moravian church with which those of us who are descendants of Friends sympathize, to banish tokens of heathenish despair from their burial service, that all things may betoken the joy and peace of the Christian entering into the reward of his Lord. And thus, as our honored friend would have wished, without ostentatious display, his bier borne by the College workmen and surrounded by his life-long and loved associates, with bloom and brightness, and Christian hope and the peace that passeth understanding breathed in the very atmosphere of that fair and tranquil afternoon, was the appropriate service said by his pupil and his friend, close beside the home of his wedded life. Before the stars, as silent guardians, had appeared, and while the sun still hung resplendent above the horizon, the long procession having reached the portion of the College cemetery beautified by his reverent care, the last rites were said, the grave was closed and flowers of his rearing covered it.

Our two venerable friends, Professor Lewis and Professor Jackson, departing so nearly together, also rest together, after a life-journey travelled side by side. Thus have we seen two pilgrims on their way. The first, listening attentively to all voices and sounds, finds in their mystery and method deep delight. To him the winter storm wails its melancholy, or resounds its sublime tokens of power and majesty, as though speaking a personal message. When the summer zephyrs whispered their bewildering secrets to his boyhood's imagination, when the thunders pealed their anthems to his mature mind, they found in him an appreciative and rapt listener. The song of the bird and the roll of the storm, nature's separate melodies and its united chorus, seemed to his sympathetic soul to resound the praises of the Creator. In his latest days he made his highest and holiest achievements. The Hebrew tongue had become to him as his own, and his utterances as to the word of God sped from land to land, illuminating deep valleys of ignorance, while his masterly exegesis of the Bible led many a captive soul out of the darkness of doubt into the marvellous light of the kingdom of Christ. But even before he reached these heights, the sounds of earth replete with mysteries of tenderness and sublimity were growing indistinct. The branches of snow-laden pines swayed in the storm but made no moan; nature reeled beneath the shock of the winter blast but its grand diapason was to his ear silent. Loving lips opened and the air was laden with greetings of reverence and affection, but the tympanum gave no record and the fondest utterances fell dead. At the close of his pilgrimage, this Christian scholar who had delighted in melody and harmony and human speech walked onward in a voiceless world. From this lower sphere, as from the upper realms of light, there was left for him but the sad assurance of the poet Addison in his favorite hymn, though with a new and striking application :

> What though in solemn silence all
> Move round this dark terrestrial ball?
> What though no real voice nor sound
> Among their radiant orbs be found?
> In reason's ear they all rejoice
> And utter forth a glorious voice.

With duty done and heart at peace, this pilgrim toil-worn in his Master's service laid him down to rest and fell " asleep in Jesus."

There were two pilgrims pressing forward and journeying ofttimes together. While he whom we have first commemorated possessed an ear attuned to sound, this fellow-pilgrim had given him of God an eye which, like the eagle's, gazed upon the sun. To him light was a perpetual study and joy. His glance, early lifted toward the stars, in thought through long years rested there. The night-watches were sweet to him because of the planets' presence, their deep and glowing mysteries, their atmospheric beauties, their exhaustless splendors. From the outset of his pilgrimage, the consideration of their movements fascinated his attention; and soon pure mathematics revealed to him celestial secrets. He knew the thrilling delight with which the solution of a difficult problem is rewarded. Above poetry and music or beauty in any other form, much as his æsthetic nature appreciated them, above all else his delight was in the Law of God as seen in principles of mathematics and laws of astronomy. He outwatched the stars to study them and burned the midnight oil in pondering the laws of light. Lifting his eyes toward the vault studded with God's suns and systems he felt flowing thence successive waves which, falling upon human orbs as upon welcome shores, told there the secrets with which they come laden to those gifted to interpret them. Astronomy was to him, as to Plato, an essential element in educating and inspiring mind and soul; pure mathematics was a sacred science, the science of ever-being, the science with which Pythagoras believed creation to begin and end its universal though voiceless oratorio. Yet light came not alone to illustrate law and to advance science, but also to reveal and to embellish earth's beauties. This pilgrim saw with joy, lights, revelations of color and of form, fair shapes of tree and shrub and flower. His affections went out and rested on them and he passed his life among them. Botany, with mathematical relations in some respects akin to those of astronomy while no less filled than is the general repertory of nature with entrancing sequences and harmonics, is also replete with instruction for mind and eye. Thus his chosen paths became more and more the walks of an expanding garden which was the outward embodiment of his thought and love. Of him it might have been said, as Wordsworth wrote of Duty,

> Flowers laugh before him in their beds,
> And fragrance in his footing treads.

And light came not merely to illustrate law and advance science and adorn nature. It spoke to him of the Divine Person who said, Let there be light. If the undevout astronomer is mad, if "the fool hath said in his heart, 'There is no God,'" light, which he loved, led this pilgrim to say in his heart of hearts, in the very spirit of the seer of old, "When I consider the heavens which Thou hast made, the moon and the stars which Thou hast ordained, then my soul proclaims thy glory, thy goodness. I bow and adore thy Being in the temple of the universe whose foundations Thou hast laid, whose irresponsible suns and systems and responsible souls Thou hast created, whose Redeemer Thou hast sent forth upon his merciful mission of re-creation."

Thus this pilgrim had loved the stars and flowers, the light of heaven and its fair reflection on the earth, the laws of pure mathematics, and the wondrous revelations of form and color which, but for light, were unseen or non-existent. At last he too was nearing his journey's end. Suddenly the fear of a horror of great darkness fell upon him, such as that which, brooding over Milton, inspired his immortal lines in praise of light, and his lament,

> These eyes, though clear
> To outward view of blemish and of spot,
> Bereft of light, their seeing have forgot;
> Nor to the idle orbs doth sight appear
> Of sun or moon or stars, throughout the year.

But this fear, which, as a threatening cloud, over-shadowed our pilgrim's pathway for a time, was mercifully removed. Sight yet remained to him and as his natural force abated he too gained the delectable mountains whence poets and prophets tell of glimpses granted them of the glories of the promised land. Then, weary and worn in the cause of duty and with no spoken word of the ravishing view which lay just before him, he, like his fellow-pilgrim, fell tranquilly into that last sleep which knows no earthly waking.

For them, the sleep of death is not the end of life. That elder pilgrim whose ear was deaf to earthly sound wakes in the realm where the believer's faith has gained the fruition of the inspired exclamation, "I HEARD as it were the voice of a great multitude and of many waters and of mighty thunderings saying, Alleluia! for the Lord God omnipotent reigneth. Let us be glad and rejoice and give honor to Him." This other pilgrim whose joy was in the light and who dreaded the on-coming of the loss of vision, wakes to the blissful realization of the meaning of those other words of the Apocalypse, "I SAW a new heaven and a new earth, and a pure river of water of life proceeding out of the throne of God and of the Lamb; and on either side, the tree of life whose leaves are for the healing of the nations; and they need no candle neither light of the sun, for the Lord God giveth them light." For them both, as for all those who love His appearing, our Saviour's blessed words, as we believe, have been fulfilled — "I go to prepare a place for you, that where I am there ye may be also."

A few months previous to the silently approaching summons, I was standing with Professor Jackson amid a throng of friends who were calling for a few words from him. Lifting his hand to request silence, he spoke somewhat as follows: "For me, the time for speech-making has passed, the day for reflection has come and for looking forward and upward. From this present life and its absorbing interests, from astronomy and the laws of matter, thought turns to the spiritual realm whither the aged are hastening. Reason and Revelation point from nature to nature's God. In quietness and confidence, faith leads the way to the better life.

The Pearl of Great Price; or, The Evangelical Creed, a Platonic Idea. Lit. & Theo. Review, Feb., 1860.
The two Schools of Philosophy. American Theological Review, Jan., 1862.
Hard Matter. Presb. and Theol. Rev., N. Y., Jan., 1863.
Emotional Element in Hebrew Translation. Methodist Quar. Review, N. Y. Four articles in 1863 and 1864.
Regula Fidei; or, The Gospel of St. John. Presb. and Theol. Rev., N. Y., Jan., 1864.
Abraham Lincoln. Hours at Home, Scribner and Co., N. Y., June, 1865.
The Bible Idea of Truth, as inseparable from the Divine Personality. Presb. and Theol. Rev., April, 1866.
Fables of Pilpay. Putnam's Magazine, N. Y., July, 1868.
Bible Words for Salvation. Presb. and Theol. Review, N. Y., Oct., 1869.
Nature of Prayer. " " April, 1870.
Ancient Oracles; or, The Primitive Greek Religion. Presb. and Theol. Review, Jan. 1871.
Jowett's Plato. Presb. and Theol. Review, Jan., 1872.
The One Human Race. Scribner's Monthly, April, 1872.
Primitive Greek Religion. Presb. and Theol. Review, July, 1872.
The Purifying Messiah; interpretation of Isaiah, 52:15. 1873.
Introduction to Farrar's Life of Christ. Wendell, Albany, 1876.
Critical Notes on the International Sunday-School Lessons on the Old Testament. Philadelphia Sunday School Times, Dec., 1876 to July, 1877.
Power and Pathos of Euripides. Harper's Monthly, Nov., 1878.
Many shorter articles; brief Reviews; Discussions in the New York Independent, Christian Intelligencer (N. Y.), Christian Statesman (Phil.), Chicago Advance, Yale Courant and others.

POSTHUMOUS MANUSCRIPTS.

Treatise on the Religious Responsibility of the State.
Figurative Language of the Bible; or, The Bible Language of the Heart.
Notes (in Arabic, Latin and English) on difficult passages in the Koran.
Notes on 463 difficult passages in the Bible.
Treatise on the Greek and Latin Metres.
Syriac Roots of the entire New Testament.
Scholia Arabica.
Many other MSS. on Biblical and Classical subjects, written chiefly in Hebrew, Greek or Latin.

ACTION OF THE TRUSTEES OF UNION COLLEGE

ON THE DECEASE OF

PROFESSOR TAYLER LEWIS, LL.D., L.H.D.

The Board of Trustees of Union College have adopted the following record expressive of their sentiments on the occasion of the decease of Professor Tayler Lewis.

Doctor Lewis was a professor in Union College for nearly thirty years. Of rare capacity as a logician and of rare acquirements as a linguist, he possessed the most valuable stores of Oriental and Classical literature.

He was an exact and erudite scholar. He was more. He knew the songs of Zion as well as the learning of Greece and Rome, and drew from all, the philosophy of human life alike of the ancients and of his nineteenth century.

With all his acquirements and capacity, he was a faithful and humble Christian whose rule of life was to follow the right wherever it seemed to him to lead. Tenacious of purpose, loving the truth for the truth's sake, he maintained his convictions in the face of all opposition unflinchingly and with ardor but without bitterness. While he hated heresy, he loved the heretic. An illustrious author and voluminous writer, his sole end and aim was that right and truth might prevail and that God should be glorified. The infirmity of his later years, which lessened his power to influence new men drew him within himself but only increased his love of learning for its own pure sake.

What his hand found to do, he did with all his might.

The influence and example of such a life is precious to all who come within its sphere. Even careless youths who failed to appreciate it when it was enacted before them in College, felt in after life its inspiration in their conscience, and with gratitude to him learned to admire and imitate its nobleness.

LIST OF THE WORKS

OF

PROFESSOR ISAAC W. JACKSON.

Elements of Conic Sections. Oliver Steele, Albany, 1838.
Elementary Treatise on Optics. Van de Bogart, Schenectady, 1852.
Elements of Trigonometry; Plane and Spherical. Barhyte, Schenectady, 1874.
Elements of Mechanics. Barhyte, Schenectady, 1874.

Association discussed; or, The Socialism of the Tribune examined. Methodist Quar. Rev., N. Y., Jan., 1848.
Chalmers. Bib. Repository, April, 1848.
Bible Ethics. " July, 1848.
The Revolutionary Spirit. Bib. Rep., Oct., 1848.
Introductory Notice to Miss Dwight's Mythology. 1849.
Astronomical Views of the Ancients. Bib. Rep., April and July, 1849.
Spirituality of the Book of Job. Bibliotheca Sacra, Andover, May and July, 1849.
Spirit of the Old Testament. Bib. Rep., Jan., 1850.
Book of Proverbs. Bib. Rep., April, 1850.
Names for Soul. " " Oct., 1850.
Review of Hickok's Rational Psychology. Biblio. Sacra., Jan. and April, 1851.
Trinitarian Letters. New Church Repository, N. Y., May, June, 1851 and Jan., March, 1852.
Three Absurdities of Modern Education. Princeton Review, April, 1851.
Editor's Table of Harper's Monthly, from Oct., 1851, to Oct., 1854, inclusive; also in 1855 and 1856; among which articles, are, in 1851, Marriage (Nov.), Time and Space, and Geology (Dec.); in 1852, Pulpit and Press (Jan.), Value of the Union (Feb.), Immensity of the Heavens (Mar.), Individuality of the Soul (Ap.), What is Education? (June), Moral Influences of the Stage (Aug.), Who is the Statesman? (Sep.), The Sabbath (Oct.); in 1853, Religious Liberty, what is it? (May), The School Question (July), What is Science? (Oct.), Woman's Rights (Nov.); in 1854, Remedies for Political Corruption (Feb.), Political Regeneration (March), Sacredness of the Human Body (Ap.), Politics of the Church (May), Union Saving (Aug.), Unity of the Race (Sep. and Oct.); in 1855, Are there more Worlds than one? (Mar.), The Self-made Man (Ap.), Conscience (Nov.); in 1866, Socrates in Prison (Ap.).
Principles or Laws of Translation; or, The True Mode of teaching Latin and Greek. New Brunswick Review, Nov., 1854.
The Old Family Bible. " " Feb., 1855.
Review of Hickok's Moral Philosophy. Presbyterian Quarterly, N. Y., Dec., 1855.
Method of teaching Greek and Latin. Barnard's Jour. of Education, Hartford; May and March, 1856.
Analysis of Sentimentalism. Mercersburg (Pa.), Review, Jan., 1857.
How Little we know. " " July, 1858.

Significance of earlier names for Deity and Soul. Young Men's Association, Albany, Dec., 1849.
Conservative Character distinguished from the Radical. Young Men's Association, Albany, 1855.
True Idea of Liberal Education. New York University Convocation, 1863.
Memoriter Instruction. " " 1864.
Knowledge of the Holy Scriptures, an indispensable element of a liberal Education. N. Y. Univ. Convocation, 1866.
The Revolutionary Spirit. Wesleyan University, 1868.
Classical Study. N. Y. Univ. Convocation, 1871.
The Moral and the Secular in Education. N. Y. Univ. Convocation, 1872.
My old Schoolmaster, " " 1875.

ARTICLES AND REVIEWS.

Method of studying the Classics. Lit. and Theol. Review, N. Y., Dec., 1838.
Great Value of the Classics as a Means of Mental Discipline. Lit. and Theol. Review, March, 1839.
The Comparative Value of Natural and Moral Science. Lit. and Theol. Review, June, 1839.
The Orphic Hymns. Iris (N. Y. Univ. Magazine), N. Y., Dec., 1840.
Study of the Heavens. " " Jan. and March, 1841.
Review of Nordheimer's Hebrew Grammar. Biblical Repository, N. Y., April, 1841.
The Ancient Metres. Iris, June, 1841.
Review of Nordheimer's Hebrew Concordance. Bib. Repository, April, 1842.
The Divine Attributes as exhibited in the Grecian Poetry; Attribute of Justice. Bib. Rep., July, 1843.
Review of " Vestiges of the Natural History of Creation." American Whig Review, N. Y., May, 1845.
Cases of Conscience. American Whig Review, July, 1845.
Human Rights. " " Oct. and Nov., 1845.
The Church Question. Biblical Repository, Jan., 1846.
Political Corruption. American Whig Review, May, 1846.
Has the State a Religion? " " March, 1846.
The Sufferings of Christ. Bib. Repository, July, 1846.
Human Justice; or, Government, a Moral Power. Bib. Rep., Jan. and April, 1847.
Classical Criticism. Knickerbocker, N. Y., Sept., 1847.
The Bible, Everything or Nothing. Bib. Rep., Jan., 1848.

ACTION OF THE TRUSTEES OF UNION COLLEGE

ON THE DECEASE OF

PROFESSOR ISAAC W. JACKSON, LL.D.

The Board of Trustees of Union College have adopted the following record, presented by Silas B. Brownell, Esq., on the occasion of the decease of Professor Isaac W. Jackson:

Professor Jackson gave his whole life to Union College. For more than fifty years he was one of her successful instructors. A devotee of his calling and our College, he was illustrious as an author of scientific text-books, and a profound scholar also of the highest branches of Pure Mathematics and the Physical Sciences.

Familiarity with abstruse science never deadened his love for humanity nor cooled his zeal for service to his fellow-men.

Communion with Nature and research in her secrets never led him into doubt or skepticism. "Through faith he understood the worlds were framed by the word of God."

That word of God which said, "Let there be light, and there was light," lightened his heart and soul and made his whole life a beautiful poem of tender charity and stainless purity.

Both literally and figuratively he dressed and kept the garden into which his Lord put him.

His loving treatment of his youthful pupils endeared him to them all; and late in life when College needed their support, he roused their enthusiasm by their affection for him.

A grateful Alma Mater values his services and celebrates his virtues while her scattered Alumni cherish his memory and, amid their grief and sorrow for their loss, reverently give thanks that such a teacher of their youth and friend of their manhood and age was so long spared to honor College by his daily life and to adorn the State and nation by the light of his example and teaching as it

Let us then be ever ready to join those whose emancipated spirits shine as the brightness of the firmament and like the stars for ever and ever!"

Beloved pupils of the graduating class, may these scenes and these lives be impressed upon your memories. In this age, conspicuous for its admiration of wealth and worldly advancement, you will need to emphasize moral qualities, as he emphasized them; to believe, as did he, that the straightforward path of Christian duty, though the narrow way, is yet the true course to honorable success and enduring happiness. One of our own poets has said, "Look not mournfully into the past; it comes not back again. Wisely improve the present; it is thine. Go forth to meet the shadowy future without fear and with a manly heart." Seek Christ for guidance, the Spirit for illumination and have faith in the Fatherhood of God. Thus He who "enlighteneth every man who cometh into the world," will lead you through this dim vale of discipline to the land of everlasting life and light.

Almighty God our heavenly Father, give us grace that we may cast away the works of darkness and put upon us the armor of light; and because through the weakness of our mortal nature we can do no good thing without thee, grant us thy grace that in keeping thy commandments we may please thee both in will and deed. May we truly repent us of our sins past, and after the good example of those thy servants who, having finished their course, do now rest from their labors, may we constantly speak the truth, boldly rebuke vice and patiently labor and if need be suffer, for the truth's sake, through Jesus Christ our Lord. Amen.

NOTE.

THE limits of time necessitated the omission of portions of the foregoing Discourses in delivery, and additional material has since been acquired.

Among the influences always cordially recognized by Doctor Lewis as affecting his literary career, should have been mentioned the sympathy and assistance rendered him in his earlier Oriental studies by Doctor Isaac Nordheimer, then Professor of Hebrew and German in the University of the City of New York and formerly Professor of Arabic, Syriac and other Oriental Languages in the University of Munich. Doctor Nordheimer talked with fluency and accuracy eleven languages. His Hebrew Grammar, "the most elaborate and philosophical in the English tongue," was the subject of Reviews by Professor Lewis and several other eminent scholars; as was also his Hebrew Concordance.

Professor Wendell Lamoroux, to whom I am herein indebted, will also supervise the printing and publication of these Discourses and will add in an Appendix material which will tend to complete this memorial tribute.

E. N. P.

APPENDIX.

LIST OF THE WORKS

OF

PROFESSOR TAYLER LEWIS.

Books.

Plato against the Atheists; or, The Platonic Theology. Harpers, N. Y., 1844.

Nature and Ground of Punishment. Putnam, N. Y., 1845.

Six Days of Creation; or, The Scriptural Cosmology. Van De Bogart, Schenectady, 1855.

The Bible and Science; or, The World Problem. Van de Bogart, Schenectady, 1856.

The Divine Human in the Scriptures. Carter and Co., N. Y., 1860.

State Rights; a Photograph from the Ruins of Ancient Greece. Weed, Parsons and Co., Albany, 1864.

The Heroic Periods in a Nation's History; An Appeal to the Soldiers of the American Armies. Baker and Godwin, N. Y., 1866.

Special Introduction to Genesis, with Commentary on chapters 1 to 11, and 37 to 50, inclusive; in Lange's Commentary. Scribner and Co., N. Y., 1868.

Rhythmical Version of Ecclesiastes, with Introduction, Dissertations and Annotations; in Lange's Commentary. Scribner and Co., N. Y., 1870.

Rhythmical Version of Job, with Introduction and Annotations; in Lange's Commentary. Scribner, Armstrong and Co., N. Y., 1874.

The Light by which we see Light; or, Nature and the Scriptures; the Vedder Lectures. Ref. Church Board of Publication, N. Y., 1875.

Memoirs of President Nott; Contributions to, and Revision. Sheldon and Co., N. Y., 1876.

Addresses.

Faith, the Life of Science. Union College Commencement, 1838.

Natural Religion, the Remains of Primitive Revelation. University of Vermont, Commencement, 1839.

The Believing Spirit. Dartmouth College Commencement, 1841.

True Idea of the State. Andover Theological Seminary, 1843.

Nature and Progress of Ideas. Union College, 1849.

shines out in the walk and conversations of the thousand of grateful Alumni who shared his instruction and his friendship and now mourn his death.

This was the heritage he craved, the reward he sought — that those whom he instructed should follow his example, imbibe his spirit and embody his precepts; that so, when they ceased to be his disciples, he might thenceforth call them friends.

His was thus a successful life. To him beyond most men, was it given to reap the harvest of his life's work. On the fiftieth anniversary of his connection with College, while men of note in church and State delighted to honor him, the boys whom he taught during those fifty years came round him once more and thus resolved:

We, the Alumni of Union College, contemplate with unmixed satisfaction the record made during the last half-century by our beloved friend and Professor, Isaac W. Jackson. We take great pleasure in congratulating him that throughout this long period of service he has retained the genuine love and veneration of the Alumni. We rejoice that this semi-centennial anniversary of his advent to Professorial work in connection with the College finds his health unimpaired, and we trust that many more years of usefulness and happiness await him.

We cherish among the most precious memories of our College days the recollection of his warm-hearted encouragement and interest in our welfare; and it is our earnest hope that the closing labors of his life may be cheered by the consciousness of possessing the confidence and love of a vast army of graduates throughout the length and breadth of the land. It is therefore

Resolved, That we greet with profound pleasure this anniversary of Professor Jackson's official connection with the College; and it is our hope and prayer that he may be long spared to the institution and the world, in the full possession of his eminent faculties of mind and his warm impulses of heart.

FORM OF BEQUEST

TO

UNION COLLEGE.

President Potter has, on several occasions, called attention to the importance of gifts and bequests to the College, of whatever kind as well as amount.

If the forty or fifty graduates yearly enrolled among our deceased, and if other friends of the institution, of Christian unity and of education, each contributed some token of remembrance; whether a pecuniary endowment; books for our Library; antiquities, photographs, single works of statuary, painting or engraving, for our Art Collection; every department of Union would soon be enabled to answer the highest demands upon its efficiency.

Every such gift, apart from its intrinsic value, not only affords special encouragement to the officers of the institution but by its example produces other benefactions perhaps greater than itself.

Already in response to these suggestions of the President, a number of bequests and gifts of interesting objects have been received and others are promised.

The most desirable form of benefaction to the College at the present time is that of contribution to its general resources, untrammeled, so far as may be, by special conditions; and since, through unacquaintance with legal details, the College may fail of the aid which would willingly have been given, its authorities have recommended that the proper title of the institution and form of bequest be published, as follows:

I give and bequeathe to the Trustees of Union College, in the town of Schenectady, in the state of New York, the

www.ingramcontent.com/pod-product-compliance
Lightning Source LLC
Chambersburg PA
CBHW031605110426
42742CB00037B/1278